Trees.
Wood.
Plants.

S82.

Trees

Carol Watson

Contents

What is a tree?

A tree is a large woody plant. It is the biggest plant in the world.

Trees are beautiful. They grow in many different shapes and sizes, but they usually have one woody stem, called a trunk.

The parts of a tree

A tree is made up of three parts which work together to make it grow. They are the crown, the trunk and the roots.

The crown

This is the top of the tree – the branches, twigs and leaves. At times it has buds and flowers, too.

3

Roots

Roots are very important for a tree. They keep it firm in the ground, and stop strong winds blowing it over. They also take in water and food from the soil, which the tree needs to stay alive and grow. This watery juice (sap) travels up the trunk to every part of the tree.

How long are roots?

Most trees have roots that spread as far underground as the tree spreads above the ground. The roots grow outwards as well as downwards, and they always grow towards water.

The trunk

The trunk is the wooden stem of the tree. It is strong enough to support all the branches in the crown. Inside the trunk are tiny tubes which carry the juicy sap around the tree.

Look closely

If you find a sawn trunk you will see a pattern of rings in the wood. A tree grows one ring for each year of its life.

What is bark?

The bark is like the skin of the tree. It protects the trunk, and stops it drying out. As old bark falls off, new bark grows underneath.

6

Branches and twigs

Branches grow from the trunk of the tree. Like the trunk, they need to be strong and are made of wood.

Twigs grow from the branches. Each twig has its own buds. Inside the buds are all the tree needs to make new leaves and flowers.

How do twigs grow?

On the very end of each twig is a
large bud, called a terminal bud.
During the winter it is covered
with thick scales. In spring the
buds burst open, and the
new shoots begin to grow.

9

Leaves

Each kind of tree has a different-shaped leaf. Most leaves are green, but sometimes the green is covered by another colour, like yellow or brown.

A tree uses its leaves to make food for itself.

How do the leaves make food?

There is water in leaves. It comes up from the roots of the tree. The green colouring in leaves uses this water, and mixes it with the air and the sun's light to make a special tree food. The food goes into the sap of the tree, and helps it to grow.

The flowers

Most trees have flowers. Some are brightly-coloured blossoms with a sweet scent. Other flowers, like catkins, are small and dull, **12** and have no scent at all.

Why do trees have flowers?

Flowers are important. They make the seeds from which new trees can grow.

How do flowers make seeds?

Some flowers are male and others are female. Male flowers have a yellow dust on them, called pollen. Female flowers need this pollen before they can make seeds. Some trees have flowers with both male and female parts.

The pollen is carried to the female flowers by insects, birds, bats, and by the wind.

13

Fruits and seeds

What is a fruit?

After the petals have fallen from a tree, a part of each old flower begins to change. It grows into a fruit. Fruits can look very different. They may be round and firm like an apple, small and soft like a berry, or hard and dry like a nut.

Peaches, acorns and elderberries are all fruits.

What does the fruit do?

Inside the fruit, the seeds of the
tree grow and ripen. The
soft fruit or hard nut
protects them.

Seeds on the move

Seeds won't sprout on a tree.
They need to grow in soil.

How do seeds reach the soil?
Animals and birds eat the ripe
fruit and drop the seeds on the
ground. Sometimes they bury
them away for the winter.

16

Other seeds are blown off the
tree by the wind. These seeds
often have wings or fluff to
carry them further through
the air.

The seeds of a conifer grow
inside a cone. On a dry day,
the cone opens, and the ripe
seeds fall onto the ground.

17

The growing seed

Each year thousands of seeds may fall
from a tree, but only a few of them will
grow and survive. A seed needs warmth,
light and water before it will grow.

1
The seed takes
in water, and
grows plumper.
It splits open.

2
A tiny root
pushes down
through the
soil.

3
A shoot
begins to
grow upwards.

4

As the stem grows, baby seed leaves begin to make food for the new plant.

5

The plant grows true leaves, like those on the adult tree.

19

Trees that lose their leaves

Trees that lose their leaves in winter are called deciduous trees. Most have broad, flat leaves.

Why do trees lose their leaves?

In autumn the weather gets colder. The days are shorter and there is less sunlight for the leaves to make food for the tree. The leaves dry out. They turn orange, red or brown and fall to the ground.

When do the leaves grow again?

The brighter light and warmer days of spring bring the tree to life. The buds open and new green leaves begin to grow.

Conifers

Trees that stay green all year are called conifers. Trees such as pines, firs, cedars and spruces are all conifers.

How are conifers different?

Conifer leaves aren't broad and flat. They are thin and waxy, with a sharp point. They are called needles. Also, the seeds of conifers don't grow on the branches. They grow inside hard, woody cones. Each type of conifer has its own kind of cone.

Where do conifers grow?

Because of their tough leaves, conifers are able to grow in colder parts of the world.

23

Tropical trees

The tropics are the warmest parts of the world. Some places, like the rainforests, are very wet. Others are drier.

Tropical rainforests

Trees in a rainforest grow very close together. They grow taller and taller to reach the bright sunlight. Some of them grow thick roots, called buttress roots, to support their trunks, and keep them firm in the ground.

Trees without rain

Some places in the tropics have no rain for months on end. Here, the trees have tough, leathery leaves to stop the hot winds drying them out.

A tree is a home

Trees provide food and nesting places for many living things.

Animals

Insects feed on the leaves or flowers of a tree. They burrow in its roots and trunk. Deer nibble the young bark. Squirrels collect acorns and nuts. Birds sleep or nest in the branches.

Plants

Climbing plants and fungi grow on the bark or around the roots. Some of these do no harm to the tree. Others take food from the tree, and slowly weaken it. This is when a tree may be attacked by disease.

Trees feed us

Like other animals, we too enjoy many of the fruits that trees provide.

Fruit trees

In summer and autumn farmers harvest fruit from their orchards – cherries, peaches, apples, pears and plums. In hotter countries, they grow citrus fruits like oranges, lemons and grapefruit.

Tropical fruits

Mangos, coconuts, dates and avocado pears are all fruits of tropical trees. Even chocolate comes from the seeds of a tree – the cacao tree.

We eat nuts, too

Trees give us nuts by the bagful – hazelnuts, pistachios, pecans and the chestnuts we eat roasted in winter.

Trees help us

What other things do trees give us?

Oxygen

The leaves change some
poisonous gases into oxygen.
We could not live without oxygen.

Wood

Tree trunks and branches are
sawn into planks, called timber.
We use timber to
make houses,
furniture, toys and
hundreds of
other things.

Paper

Paper is wood
that has been
mashed to a pulp.

30

Cork

Cork comes from the
bark of the cork oak tree.

Rubber

We make rubber from the
sap of the rubber tree.

31

Index

HarperCollins Children's Books

A Division of HarperCollins Publishers Ltd, 77–85 Fulham Palace Road, Hammersmith, London W6 8JB

First published 1994 in the United Kingdom

Copyright © HarperCollins*Publishers* 1994

Prepared by *specialist publishing services* 090 857 307

3 5 7 9 10 8 6 4 2

ISBN 0 00 196541 7

A CIP record is available from the British Library

Illustrated by Peter Bull

Photographs by A–Z Botanical Collection: 8, 10, 12/13, 17, 31; Bernard Annebicque/SYGMA: 31; Dr Basil Booth/Geoscience: 2/3, 16, 29; Comstock: 22/23; Billie Cook/Life File: 28; J Morrison/Life File: 13; Lionel Moss/Life File: 25; John I Ray/TSW: 20/21; Jan Shuttle/Life File: 7; Nicola Sutton/Life File: 31; Andy Teare/Life File: 24/25; Flora Torrance/Life File: 30/31.

Series editor: Nick Hutchins; Editing: Claire Llewellyn; Design: Eric Drewery/Susi Martin; Picture research: Lorraine Sennett

Printed and bound in Hong Kong